HONG KONG
PAST & PRESENT

Hong Kong:
Past & Present

Published by:
FormAsia Books Limited
706, Yu Yuet Lai Building
45, Wyndham Street
Central. Hong Kong
www.formasiabooks.com

Published 2003
ISBN: 962-7283-57-6
Text and photographs
© FormAsia Books Limited

Main text by Sherry Lee
Historic Perspectives by Peter Moss
Designed by Ian Leung
FormAsia Marketing by Eliza Lee
Photography from FormAsia Books Archive
Printed in Hong Kong
Printed by Noble World Printing Company Limited
Film separations by Skyart Graphic Company Limited

HONG KONG
PAST&PRESENT

Sherry Lee

FormAsia

PAST&PRESENT

Sherry Lee

In the long, hot summer of 1967, a San Po Kong plastic flower factory strike, triggered by local Communist influence, spawned riots, leaving 51 people dead and injuring thousands. Hong Kong was turned into a battleground – at night, hundreds of people attacked police with knives, stones, home-made bombs, kerosene and sharpened water pipes; police fought back with shields, batons and gas masks; and people were stabbed to death.

It was the summer of my birth – 28 September in a tiny Jockey Club clinic in Sheung Shui.

My parents named me Lee Man Nei, after a Chinese singer at the time. As a child, I loved singing and hoped one day to become a singer.

Like most of Hong Kong's early residents, my parents were refugees. Troubled times had forced them into an itinerant existence.

When the Japanese invaded Hong Kong in 1941, my grandparents, with their six-month-old son, fled to grandfather's home village of Huidong in Guangdong Province. Three years later, my mother was born there.

When Japanese soldiers invaded my father's village in Sha Tau Kok - close to the Hong Kong – China border, he also fled, to Guangzhou City.

During the war his aunt couldn't afford to care for him, so he was sent to a local orphanage. He always maintained his life wouldn't have been so unpleasant had his elder sister not abandoned him for the Communist revolution in China. Like thousands of other 'hot-blooded youngsters', she and her lover joined the Communists and fought against the KMT for Chairman Mao.

> Like thousands of other 'hot-blooded youngsters', she and her lover joined the Communists and fought against the KMT for Chairman Mao.

After the war father returned to Hong Kong. He lived with his uncle, a primary school headmaster whose family occupied a house linked to the school. Father complained about uncle, who cared little for him and didn't provide him with enough food. To earn his board, he worked as a cleaner for the school.

My grandparents got wind that the British military needed labourers to help build the Shek Kong military camp, together with living quarters on the slopes of Tai Mo Shan (Foggy Hill). They successfully applied to work on the project and moved to a nearby valley.

Tai Mo Shan loomed large between Tsuen Wan and Kam Tin and was linked to both by Route Twisk. The area was mountainous, with many birds and few residents. My grandparents, with four other families, became the valley's only dwellers. By day they built army bungalows, while at night they lived contentedly in shacks they had built themselves. Additional people arrived to help build the military camp, and the village population grew, becoming a small squatter settlement.

While grandfather laid drainage for the army quarters, grandmother tended the family pigs and chickens, and gave birth to four additional children.

Once construction of the army camp was completed grandfather went to work as a handyman in Lok Ma Chau police station, where he was responsible for its public areas, the daily raising of the British flag at sunrise and its lowering at 6 p.m., and polishing policemen's black boots.

Mother, who was then six, accompanied her parents on their return to Hong Kong, settling in a Tai Po village. Like most other children in Hong Kong at the time, she had to walk to and from school rather than enjoy the luxury of a school bus. After school, she scavenged bread crusts and potato skins from bins outside the army camps to feed the family pigs. Need forced her to leave primary school and seek work in a garment factory in Fanling at the age of sixteen. It was there that she met father, who was by then a Customs and Excise officer.

Grandmother recalls that father liked my mother because she 'worked hard'. He told me that when he first started courting mother, she was a typical country girl. "I asked her to the movies," he recalls, laughing, "When she appeared, she wasn't wearing any shoes. I thought 'how odd that this girl doesn't wear shoes!'" My mother said she did it on purpose because she wasn't really impressed by father at the time, and accepted the invitation only after his repeated requests. Mother later quit her job to become an *amah* for the soldiers' families. And she eventually married father because grandmother claimed his government job was as secure as an 'iron rice bowl'.

Our village was named Lui Kung Tin, or Field of the Thunder Grandfather, because of frequent thunderstorms in the vicinity. Mother always feared our home, with its flimsy wooden walls and zinc roof, would collapse during a typhoon. I wasn't in the least scared. I felt comforted and secure at home.

It was a small house with two bedrooms. My parents slept in one room, little larger than their bed, while I shared the other room, furnished with bunks, with my two brothers. I flipped a coin for the top bunk with my elder brother, crying every time I lost. On the lower bunk I'd hang up an orange blanket to create a wall behind which my younger brother and I would hide.

The house had a large front terrace and a rear garden filled with plants and trees, the envy of other

> Our village was named Lui Kung Tin, or Field of the Thunder Grandfather, because of frequent thunderstorms in the vicinity.

village children. Every afternoon friends would come to our garden to plant flowers, climb trees and swing on ropes dangling from branches. Ever since I was little, I had loved climbing trees and I could run faster than most of the children in the neighbourhood.

With other children, I'd swim daily in a nearby reservoir and we'd jump off a bridge, about as high as a two-story building, into the deep water below. We would also teeter our way, like acrobats, across a narrow black water pipe spanning the river. It was exciting and I never fell in. People said children who grew up in the New Territories were more aggressive and optimistic than city children. That was me then…and that's me today.

In 1962, Hong Kong people began to experience water shortages, prompting the government to sign an agreement with China in 1964 to purchase water between the months of October and June each year from China's East River. In 1974, and again in 1977, water levels in local reservoirs dropped to alarmingly low levels and many people were rationed, receiving water once every four days. People with buckets and tin cans would queue for hours at water hydrants in the streets. But water was supplied non-stop to our village. Like others, my father laid long pipes all the way to the top of a clear stream, supplying us with fresh and sweet water at all hours during the drought, however this didn't stop mother from teaching us never to waste a drop of water.

Despite father's position as a Customs officer, it wasn't easy keeping a family of five in Hong Kong during the 70s. Mother grew vegetables and raised hens to supplement our living. I was scared to feed the chickens or collect their eggs because of our ill-tempered rooster that always attacked if one got too close. Regardless of his persistent assaults, farm life was an adventure, and introduced us to many strange things. Once under a plank we found a nest of baby mice. They were so tiny and pink and their eyes had not yet opened.

During the 1970s, some in the village earned additional income by assembling plastic flowers for factories similar to that run by tycoon Li Ka-shing at Diamond Hill, while many in the city worked in textile and garment factories.

This was the golden era of Hong Kong – benefiting from booming international trade and prospering as a 're-exporter' for China, which then had few ties with foreign countries. Hong Kong, which in the 70s had an economic growth rate of 10 percent, became a major centre for international finance. Thanks to this strong economy, the then Governor, Sir Murray MacLehose was determined to push forward improvements in the living standards of Hong Kong residents. Included in his ambitious plans was a 10-year programme to resettle 1.8 million people from hillside squatter shacks into public housing as a precaution against further destructive typhoons and devastating squatter fires.

> **In 1974, and again in 1977, water levels in local reservoirs dropped to alarmingly low levels and many people were rationed, receiving water once every four days.**

Across the border, destitute Chinese heard of Hong Kong's rapid growth and hordes of people arrived daily, either by swimming or traversing mountains and valleys evading border patrols. In a single month in 1979, over 11,000 illegal immigrants were apprehended at the border.

Our family also experienced this refugee tide – one day mother took sets of new clothes to two mainland relatives. She hurriedly made them change into more urban-looking clothes so they wouldn't be spotted by the police, and brought them to grandmother's home. As the man arrived, he said: "Oh, how good it is, now that we have reached paradise."

With both parents working, my elder brother and I inevitably arrived home to a locked house after school, which meant having to wait on the doorstep for father to come home. Once he was upset to find me sitting alone, bitten by mosquitoes from head to toe.

I remember father as tall and handsome, playing Beatles and Bee Gees songs on his old hi-fi when we were small. A typical government officer, he speaks in a clear and orderly manner with a stern look on his face. But he was certainly different from some of his colleagues, who at the time were on the take. In the 1970s, Governor MacLehose introduced the Independent Commission Against Corruption to combat this curse in our society. Scores of government officers were tried then jailed, while many fled overseas. My father, who witnessed these events, often said: "If I had taken bribes, I too would

be in jail and your life today would be that much poorer."

Like other civil servants of the Hong Kong Government, whose policies were frequently in conflict with those of Communist China, father dared not return to the mainland for fear of arrest.

When we were older, mother returned to work as an *amah* for $70 a month. Brother and I missed her, and would often visit her at her work in the *'gweipau hon'* (western women's Public Works Department bungalows.)

"My girl," mother said in her limited English, introducing me to her British employer, who had brown hair and a kind smile. My mother, slim and beautiful, had lovely smiling eyes and always wore a ponytail.

At home I would comb her hair, and she would correct my English. I loved long hair as a child. A barber used to come to our village to give children haircuts for five cents a head. He always cut my hair short. I really hated it and cried. Mother would placate me by saying: "But you look like a flight stewardess." Mother was instrumental in my education. She would hold a book up, hiding the phrases, and ask me to spell the words in English, or else read aloud.

At Chinese New Year, mother would bring us to Kowloon and Hong Kong Island to buy new clothes. I loved Apple denim skirts, which were very trendy. I also loved the cross-harbour ferry rides, which were exciting but scary because of the deep, dark harbour water. Mother couldn't swim, and

> **Scores of government officers were tried then jailed, while many fled overseas.**

I wondered how, if the ferry sank, I could save her. The thought of losing mother was terrifying, and tears would prick my eyes.

Another reason to be in the city was to visit grandmother. During the civil war in China the Communists had banned the export of pigs to the British colony, so grandmother perceptively made a living by selling pigs. But in the 60s, the mainland government suddenly changed tack and lifted the ban. Pork prices plummeted, forcing grandmother to abandon the business. Instead she turned her hand to construction work, later becoming a cook and then a hawker, a common way of life for refugees in those days.

Earning a living necessitated that my grandparents live apart, grandfather stayed in our village and travelled to Lok Ma Chau, where he worked at the police station and grandmother rented a $30-a- month room in the city. They would meet a few times a year at Chinese festivals, or when grandmother brought home her monthly earnings.

Being with grandmother in her tiny room with its lone bunk-bed and diminutive window, separated from others by wooden boards, with access to a wet, dirty kitchen and a toilet shared with five families, made me uneasy. On a few occasions mother and I stayed overnight in her cramped quarters. Showering in the toilet was an awful experience, while the intrusive morning traffic noise was a constant reminder that we were in the heart of the city. I delighted in the sound of the city, but also found it alien.

As a traditional Chinese, grandmother loved boys, sons-in-law and male relatives, a love underscored by the fact that she had lost a son to the evils of drugs. Heroin was the most common drug in Hong Kong in the 1960s. Dealers would lure teenagers into taking drugs and then turn them into pushers. Drug abuse quickly spread through the housing estates and villages. This was how 'small uncle', grandmother's youngest son, became addicted.

> **Grandmother loved boys, sons-in-law and male relatives, a love underscored by the fact that she had lost a son to the evils of drugs.**

Villagers put it down to bad *fung shui*, saying it was because our village, situated below Tai Mo Shan, was located in a valley and didn't receive positive energy. One day when I was about seven, I returned home to find grandmother sobbing and a Hakka neighbour chanting words I couldn't understand. I learnt that uncle had been murdered. His body was discovered inside a rainwater tunnel not far from our village. Years later, grandmother seemed to have recovered from her sadness. I haven't, and to this day remain angry over it.

I was envious of my elder brother, who could easily attract the kind of attention I craved. Once, during a visit to grandmother, I felt everyone was paying him too much attention. Despite my obvious displeasure, mother and grandmother ignored me. As we were walking in Sham Shui Po, I went off by myself. Later, the police found me and escorted me to their station. I couldn't remember what I told them, but a policewoman remarked how calm I was

8

during the ordeal. Mother reported me missing but the police advised her I was safe at the station. Relieved, she took me home without a scolding.

I can't remember my brother's reaction but I know he cared about me. Neighbours said that when we were small, and often late for the school bus, he would call "*mui mui* (sister), faster." Bus 51 from Tsuen Wan was the village's link with the outside world – but it was irregular and we often had to wait for it for at least half an hour. Every morning, we children would be waiting anxiously at the bus stop. We could tell from its groaning noise that it was halfway up the hill, and we would cry out "the bus is coming".

I invariably fell asleep on the ride to school, with elder brother having to wake me. Twice however, whether on purpose or not, he left me asleep. Everyone had disembarked, and I woke up long after the bus had left the school stop. I leapt off at the next stop and was nervously walking to school along the bus route when brother came looking for me.

I studied at the Yuen Long Government Primary School. In each classroom a portrait of the Queen hung on the wall. Looking back, I didn't like school. I found interaction between students and teachers lacking. I was of a curious, inquisitive nature and constantly asked questions. A teacher once reprimanded me and ordered me to remain silent. I did badly in my studies and my mother warned my elder brother that if we failed in our examinations, we would have to move out of the village house. One day at Primary Two when I was handed my school report, I happily showed it to my brother during an interval, thinking I had scored well. "You're dead, your average mark is red. You've failed," he said.

At home, mother said we had to move. I was scared, wondering where we might end up. As younger brother was still an infant, elder brother and I packed our clothes and departed to grandmother's house. Crying all the way, we met mother's younger sister, Aunt Mai Shim, who sent us back home to mother.

School didn't improve much over the years and I was once second to last in a final examination. My English up to that time was atrocious, but when I was about ten I started to take a keen interest, thanks to two sisters, Siu Ying and Fung Ying, who lived nearby. Their parents ran a grocery store and supplied fresh eggs and vegetables to English-speaking families in the military camp. The sisters would knock on the door of the families asking if they needed grocery supplies. They taught me simple English phrases and encouraged me to practice them.

First, I accompanied them to learn the ropes. Then, I ventured out alone. It was gratifying to know customers actually understood my English. Apart from meeting mother's nice employer, this became my first direct contact with western people. Later, along with my younger brother, I went to the playground exclusively for children

> I invariably fell asleep on the ride to school, with elder brother having to wake me. Twice however, whether on purpose or not, he left me asleep.

9

living in the military camp. There I practiced my English, using phrases like "you and I – friend". Some of the children played with us, while others were unfriendly.

Festivals in our village were unforgettable. At Chinese New Year, my city cousin would come to celebrate. I called her 'cousin Ha'. She had two ponytails and thin lips. Everyone said she was 'beautiful and gentle', implying that with short hair and a tanned skin I wasn't, instead being considered rural and rough.

Although envious of cousin Ha, I was excited when she visited. She and her family lived in a flat in a public housing estate. Their home was tiny, with little more than bunk beds, television set, fridge and toilet. Cousin looked trendy and wore shoes with heels. Once her mother generously gave me a pair of white-heeled shoes. I was so excited and immediately wore them to show off to my neighbours.

On New Year's Eve, cousin and I, in preparation for the New Year, would place our new clothes neatly on a chair next to our bed. Out of sheer excitement I couldn't sleep and hoped that morning would soon arrive. As the roosters started to crow and the sky lightened, we would get up, dress quickly in our new clothes and then parade into the village centre, competing for attention with the other children.

At Mid-Autumn Festival we lit red, blue, pink or purple paper lanterns on our terrace and the family would gather in the courtyard. We would admire the glow of the moon, enjoy fruits and specially baked moon cakes. Looking at the moon, my mother told me the love story between a cowherd and a weaving girl who was once a princess.

One day, the youngest of the seven celestial princesses in heaven, who lived in the moon, secretly fell in love with the poor but honest Ngau Nong, a cowherd on the Earth. She escaped, and descended to Earth to meet him. The couple lived happily together, the cowherd working the fields and the princess weaving at home. But one day the celestial empress traced her to the village where she and the cowherd lived. Angry, she punished them, decreeing that they could only see each other once a year, this being the seventh day of the seventh month, usually around the Mid-Autumn Festival. On this day cowherd and weaving girl would meet on a bridge in the moon, and people on Earth would light lanterns to guide them. On those occasions father was rarely with us; he would invariably be playing *mahjong* with the neighbours.

In the early 1980s, Hong Kong experienced traumatic changes. Britain and China started negotiations for the handover of Hong Kong to the People's Republic, scheduled for 1997. After a meeting with Chinese leader Deng Xiaoping, British Prime Minister Margaret Thatcher slipped down the stairs

> **As the roosters started to crow and the sky lightened, we would get up, dress quickly in our new clothes and then parade into the village centre, competing for attention with the other children.**

at the Great Hall of the People, hurting Hong Kong more than herself we felt. Those who saw it on TV related it to the downward slide of Hong Kong. Share prices plummeted, and the migration of people from Hong Kong to Canada, Australia and the United States began.

In the 1980s Hong Kong experienced unprecedented growth. Tycoon Li Ka-shing made a fortune building high rise apartments, becoming Hong Kong's richest man. The Mass Transit Railway project was partially completed in 1979, to become the major mode of transport in Hong Kong. The outmoded coal-fired Kowloon Canton Railway trains were replaced in 1983 by an electrified line. Sailing junks slowly disappeared from Victoria Harbour. Reclaimed sea fronts shortened ferry trips between Kowloon and Hong Kong Island. Much of pre-war Hong Kong gave way to frenzied redevelopment, and the classic granite building of the Hongkong and Shanghai Bank in Central was replaced by a glass-and-metal high rise.

The tide of migration slowed, while scores of mainlanders continued to flock to Hong Kong. Like our parents and grandparents, they came to seek a better life. The local population was increasing rapidly and soon there were almost six million people, many living in public housing flats.

In the New Territories, rice fields became construction sites, and eventually high-rise towers. Spanish-style villas started appearing in the late

In the New Territories, rice fields became construction sites, and eventually high-rise towers.

1970s and the six new towns in the New Territories, laid out by Governor MacLehose's government, became densely populated.

Soon, it was June 1997 and the 99-year lease of the New Territories, which China had been forced to sign with Britain in 1898, came to an end. The change of administration allowed the new Hong Kong Government to award the Grand Bauhinia Medal to leftist Yeung Kwong in October 2001, despite the fact that he was the ringleader of the 1967 riots which claimed 51 lives and injured thousands of people. The Basic Law became Hong Kong's post-1997 constitution.

And in the interim I didn't become a singer, despite my love of performing as a child. Instead I became a journalist, which helped me understand and love Hong Kong even more. It also allowed me to witness at close hand the many changes taking place.

On the night of 30, June 1997, as Hong Kong was being returned to China in a ceremony at the Convention Centre I found myself in a newsroom observing history being played out before my eyes on television.

The Union Jack was finally lowered and the red flag of China raised. Sitting close by was a Hong Kong-born English reporter who wept. I understood her feelings as I too was saddened by the departure of the British. It was like saying goodbye to an old friend.

It was a time of personal conflict within me. Lingering in my mind was the June 1989 military crackdown at Tiananmen Square, in which hundreds were killed. At the same time I was happy that we were returning to our motherland after more than a century and a half of colonial rule. During the playing of China's national anthem, as the flag reached the top of the pole, I clapped my hands.

I felt sorry to see Chris Patten and his family depart on the British royal yacht. It had been raining and the family was in tears. Patten was the only governor who had made an impression on me, and I thank him for bringing democracy to Hong Kong. I feel that if he had stayed longer, Hong Kong would be a different place today.

> **I felt sorry to see Chris Patten and his family depart on the British royal yacht. It had been raining and the family was in tears.**

After 1997, most of my western colleagues and friends quit Hong Kong - partly because the city had lost its historic charm. The presence of the international media was much reduced. Hong Kong now lacked controversy, providing fewer opportunities for good stories. I was saddened by their departure.

A Chinese colleague told me she had no confidence in China because of its control over the press. She also departed. But I remain much more optimistic. The more problems that befall a society, the more I have to engage myself. If journalists capitulate, who then will cry out for change?

I love working in the media – as a teenager I loved writing and as an adult even more so. My job consumes me and I will use it to serve Hong Kong. I hope Hong Kong retains its freedom of speech, so that people can continue their high standard of living.

Recently, during the Mid-Autumn Festival, I returned to Tai Mo Shan. Our village remains unchanged, except that the neighbours have improved their shabby homes into neat houses. The *gweipau hon* are still there although the occupants

are no longer British but mainland soldiers from the People's Liberation Army.

Grandmother's house has changed considerably. The pigpens are long gone, the ugly cement floor has been covered by smooth tiles, and the grassy backyard is now a modern garden. Sadly, my family home had fallen into disrepair. Several neighbours wanted to buy it, but mother declined to sell. Recently, younger brother Kin got involved, turning it into a brick house with a brand new zinc roof. Each weekend he and close friends work on improving it further, and I am happy to see Kin so dedicated.

Father retired in 1994. He no longer fears returning to China and like thousands of retired Hong Kong residents, has bought an inexpensive house in Guangdong Province and lives there part of the time. Mother spends time in Shenzhen with friends. Elder brother Hong has given up his Bruce Lee weapons. Aged twenty-nine, Kin is a technician, who repairs drinks vending machines and lives with my parents in Tai Po. We are in close contact and care for each other.

Grandmother has silver-grey hair and her face is finely wrinkled. She continues to sell fruit under the staircase of a Sham Shui Po building. We would all like her to retire but she remains undecided promising us, "after this year". She speaks kindly, is always so pleased to see me and we remain in touch. Cousin Ha, still in vogue in high heels, though she no longer wears ponytails, is a mature woman who wears her hair at shoulder length and lives with her little boy in Ap Lei Chau.

As for myself, I moved out of the family home and live with Sang, my boyfriend, but I miss the daily interaction with my family and I have never had the long hair I dreamt of as a child.

> **Grandmother has silver-grey hair and her face is finely wrinkled. She continues to sell fruit under the staircase of a Sham Shui Po building.**

The classic panorama of Hong Kong, scrolled like an indelible signature across the mind of the beholder, was always viewed from the north, preferably across the harbour from a vantage point on the Kowloon peninsula. Whatever might change in the foreground, with junks giving way to jetfoils, and elegant colonnades to steel and glass monoliths, the mountains endured.

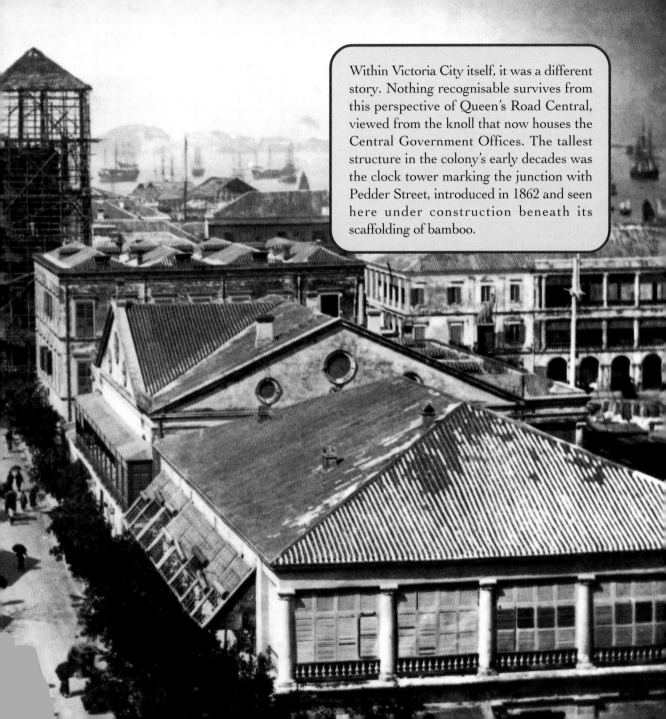

Within Victoria City itself, it was a different story. Nothing recognisable survives from this perspective of Queen's Road Central, viewed from the knoll that now houses the Central Government Offices. The tallest structure in the colony's early decades was the clock tower marking the junction with Pedder Street, introduced in 1862 and seen here under construction beneath its scaffolding of bamboo.

The clock tower barely outlasted (by just one year) the inauguration in 1912 of an even taller structure, in the form of the distinguished new Supreme Court. Though still surviving, as the home of the Legislative Council, the grandeur of the latter now seems greatly diminished by the ramparts of subsequent development.

Once successive reclamations established Statue Square as fulcrum of commerce, it followed that the city's most favoured locations were those fronting this plaza. Though the statues have largely disappeared, the Cenotaph still stands as monument to Hong Kong's war dead. Overlooking this public arena since its relocation there in 1897, the Hong Kong Club has undergone a further transformation.

The inscription on the Cenotaph, dedicated to 'The Glorious Dead, 1914-1918, 1939-1945,' commemorates not just those in military service, many of whom died defending Hong Kong, but also students, doctors and nurses who fought across South China in support of the British Army Aid Group, together with Communist guerrillas of the East River Column who joined in the struggle against Japanese invasion.

West of Statue Square stood Queen's Building, inaugurated in 1899 to symbolize Hong Kong's unbridled aspirations for the 20th century. Based on the premise that no one work embodies all aspects of style, its architecture was virtually a textbook illustration of derivative forms that somehow combined to achieve a harmonious whole. In 1963 it was replaced by the Mandarin Hotel.

When it opened its doors in 1849, just seven years after the inception of Hong Kong as a British crown colony, St. John's Cathedral's elevation above the city removed it to a higher plane of civic accomplishment. Today it is overlooked by a welter of development that has swept past it to claim the still higher ground of the Mid Levels.

Even though sword scabbards have ceased clattering along tiled floors, and its portico no longer serves for last-minute adjustments of epaulettes and other martial insignia, while the bride coyly bides her time, St. John's Cathedral remains the favoured setting for matrimonial occasions, where the red of the traditional Chinese wedding gown has given way to a dazzling uniformity of whiteness.

Reoccupying Government House, under a newly-added tower of suspiciously Nipponese persuasion, post-war colonial governors balked at this reminder of Japanese occupation. But impartial observers decreed it a great architectural improvement. So the tower has remained, long after the last colonial incumbent departed for good, leaving little more than echoes to resonate in a mausoleum to an imperial past.

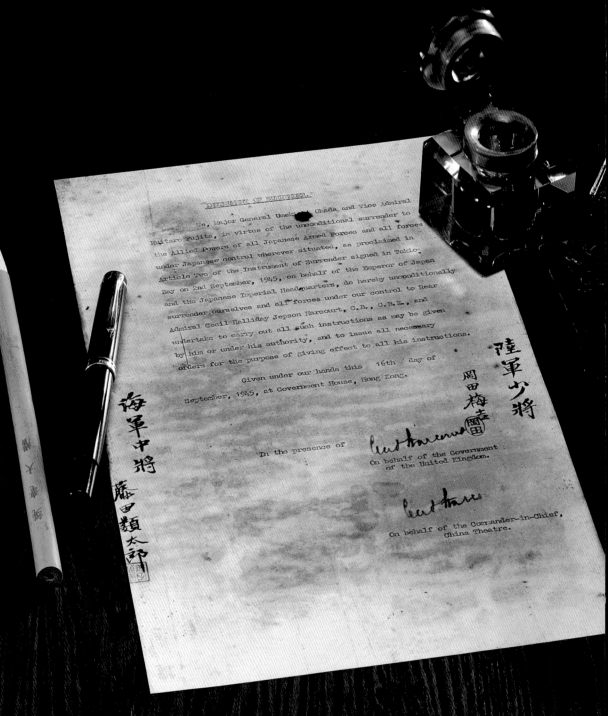

INSTRUMENT OF SURRENDER.

We, Major General Umekichi Okada and Vice Admiral
Ruitaro Fujita, in virtue of the unconditional surrender to
the Allied Powers of all Japanese Armed Forces and all forces
under Japanese control wherever situated, as proclaimed in
Article Two of the Instrument of Surrender signed in Tokio
Bay on 2nd September, 1945, on behalf of the Emperor of Japan
and the Japanese Imperial Headquarters, do hereby unconditionally
surrender ourselves and all forces under our control to Rear
Admiral Cecil Halliday Jepson Harcourt, C.B., C.B.E., and
undertake to carry out all such instructions as may be given
by him or under his authority, and to issue all necessary
orders for the purpose of giving effect to all his instructions.

Given under our hands this   16th   day of
September, 1945, at Government House, Hong Kong.

In the presence of

On behalf of the Government
of the United Kingdom.

On behalf of the Commander-in-Chief,
China Theatre.

On learning of Emperor Hirohito's surrender speech in Tokyo, the British moved quickly to regain control of Hong Kong. As soon as he received word of Japanese capitulation, Franklin Gimson, Hong Kong's colonial secretary, left the prison camp at Stanley and declared himself the territory's acting governor. At a ceremony staged in Government House, British Rear Admiral Sir Cecil Harcourt formally accepted the Japanese surrender document.

A surrender document of another kind was the Sino-British Joint Declaration, signed by the heads of the two governments in Beijing on 19 December 1984, under which China resumed sovereignty over Hong Kong. On 27 May 1985, the two governments exchanged instruments of ratification, under which the Sino-British Joint Declaration formally went into effect.

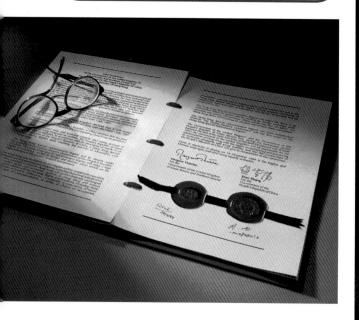

Almost exactly 30 years before the 1997 handover, an offshoot of China's cultural revolution, in the summer of 1967, led to riots, demonstrations and bombings that briefly threatened Hong Kong's continued existence as a British crown colony. The Bank of China bristled with loudspeakers, blaring revolutionary propaganda that failed to put players of the Hong Kong Cricket Club off their stroke.

Inaugurated in 1990, seven years before Hong Kong was due to return to the motherland, the new Bank of China rose like a portent of vastly more exciting things to come. Its architect, I.M. Pei, is the son of the bank's first Hong Kong manager of the Nationalist era. Those who found his concept lacking in Chinese elements were told "I didn't design a pagoda".

The architecture of early Hong Kong was calculated to leave no doubt as to its durability. No mere makeshift façade of transient authority, here was the very essence of permanence, carved into ornately porticoed brick and granite. And yet, as this early manifestation of the Hong Kong Bank would soon attest, the city has remained forever seized with dissatisfaction at its accomplishments, recreating itself over and over again.

Like a phoenix bent on self-incineration, in order to arise from its ashes in ever brighter raiment, "The Bank" underwent major surgery with each metamorphosis. When its 1935 variant was surpassed by its immediate neighbours, the Bank of China and the Standard Chartered Bank, it opted for more extreme measures by commissioning Sir Norman Foster to produce a design quite unlike anything Hong Kong had seen before.

Motorists are among Hong Kong's greatest opportunists. When the Hong Kong Cricket Club was eventually moved to Wong Ngai Chung Gap, in 1975, cars flocked to the once sacred turf to seek temporary refuge from on-street parking meters. Completed in 1962, the Hongkong Hilton became a prime example of transient architecture by surviving a mere 30 years before demolition, in 1992, to make way for the Cheung Kong Center.

A ready guide to Hong Kong's meteoric growth of traffic and population can be derived from a comparison of 'before and after' pictures along the main thoroughfares through Central District, such as Des Voeux Road, where the frequency of both trams and pedestrians has increased manifold over the years since rickshaws and sedan chairs provided the principal means of conveyance.

Once employed as manifestations of civic loyalty to king and empire, in the heyday of imperial occasions, Hong Kong trams have now become travelling billboards of commercial advertising, promoting airlines, tourist destinations, electronic gadgetry and just about everything except the tramways themselves, whose entrenched popularity as the cheapest available means of transport ensures they never lack passengers.

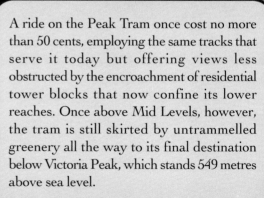

A ride on the Peak Tram once cost no more than 50 cents, employing the same tracks that serve it today but offering views less obstructed by the encroachment of residential tower blocks that now confine its lower reaches. Once above Mid Levels, however, the tram is still skirted by untrammelled greenery all the way to its final destination below Victoria Peak, which stands 549 metres above sea level.

In contrast to the frequently altered profiles of the rival banks, other structures aligned around Statue Square proved more tenacious in holding out against the tides of progress. The adjoining Queen's and Prince's Buildings both survived approximately sixty years, while the Hong Kong Club lasted from 1897 to 1981. Most enduring of all is the Supreme Court, now listed as a heritage building.

Even more striking than the upward growth of its skyline has been the outward expansion of the city's foreshore. Viewed from the Peak, the demarcation between sea and land, along the north coast of Hong Kong Island, now appears considerably less concave than it did a mere forty years ago. The waterfront from Central to Causeway Bay has since advanced far into the harbour.

The narrowing of the channel between the island and Kowloon has greatly abbreviated the distance covered in the ceaseless harbour crossings traversed by the ambidextrous Star Ferry vessels, equally adept at coming and going because they make no distinction between bow and stern. While the extended funnels of early models resembled clumsy attempts at cigarette advertising, the overall shape and size have remained much the same.

KING'S BUILDING

UNION BUILDING

CANADIAN PACIFIC

Riddled with archways and deeply recessed balconies, the city's earlier mercantile premises invited speculation as to what went on within those shaded interiors, where perhaps typewriters and ticker tapes had replaced quill pens and ledger books below the whirling blades of electric fans. Today all conjecture is rebuffed by gigantic mirrored faces, endlessly reflecting each other in mutual admiration. Chater House, built where Swire House formerly occupied the site of its preceding Union House, embodies an image of Jardine House, originally known as Connaught Centre.

The last post for the venerable Central Post Office was sounded in 1976, when its Indo-Saracen battlements offered inadequate defence against the onslaughts of rapacious developers, bent on transforming the site into yet another curtain-walled high-rise of maximized floor space and minimized architectural interest. Ironically its replacement, located on reclaimed land further out to sea, embodies an echo of those lost columns and arches.

"Spectacle was an important tool of imperial dominion, expressed in architecture, in ritual, in bearing, in military display, in the show of history…" wrote Jan Morris, in her book "Fisher's Face". She might thus have described the officers of Hong Kong's military establishment, or its police force housed in the granite fastness of the Central Police Station in Hollywood Road.

1919

HONG · KONG · POLICE ·

63

Ritual and pageantry of quite another form attended the cycle of celebrations that marked the festive seasons of the traditional lunar calendar, well before the arrival of the earliest colonizers in 1841. Man Mo Temple in Hollywood Road, built in 1847, is among the most richly decorated but by no means oldest of shrines, some of which are of considerably earlier vintage.

For the dash and panache of sheer spectacle, it would be hard to beat the feverish anticipation that descended upon Happy Valley on race day. It was an atmosphere far removed from the more virulent fevers that had taken the lives of the earliest colonial settlers, before strenuous drainage works dispelled malarial swamps to facilitate the establishment of Hong Kong's principal recreational activity.

Having immortalized it in his song Mad Dogs and Englishmen, it was inevitable that Noel Coward should fulfil at least one of the functions he described in his reference to Hong Kong. In Hong Kong, he claimed, they strike a gong and fire off a noonday gun, to reprimand each inmate who's in late. The gun is still fired, every day, in a garden on Gloucester Road, across from the Excelsior Hotel.

St. Paul's was an orphanage when this photograph (left) was taken in the 1930's. The orphans had gone, and the building had been extensively remodeled, when the later photograph was taken to recreate the mood of the original. But the tiled floor had survived, as had the very same nuns, now supervising a much later generation of children – this time schoolchildren rather than orphans.

The oldest tertiary education institution in Hong Kong, the University of Hong Kong occupies 49 hectares of land that stretch along the north-western slopes of Hong Kong Island, between 50 and 150 metres above sea level. Its earliest buildings, housing faculties of medicine and engineering, date from its inauguration in 1913. Remarkably – for Hong Kong – the background of green hills remains almost as verdant as it appeared then.

By 1917 – four years after it took in its first students – the university claimed a total enrolment of two hundred. Today it enrolls over 14,000 in nine faculties. Academic gowns and mortarboards have replaced the pantaloons and cheongsams of earlier generations, while unrestrained exuberance, rather than the severity of suppressed enthusiasm, now marks the mood of graduation day.

Tatterdemalion latticework of typhoon-ravaged sail notwithstanding, the traditional junk, once so common in Hong Kong waters, imposed an emblematic stamp upon the panorama. Like the vermilion seal on an artist's scroll, it instantly defined the very substance of Hong Kong. Its streamlined successors, looking as if they would be more at home in a James Bond movie, obscure more than complement their background.

The typhoons that once emptied the bustling Central Praya, and wrought havoc among the fishing population, are still capable of stranding giant cargo vessels. An engine of destruction dreadful to behold, the typhoon is also a phenomenon with which the territory, from its earliest decades of bitter experience, is now more than amply organized to withstand.

Disasters of other species have also been inflicted upon the floating population in Aberdeen harbour. In the course of final preparations, prior to its scheduled opening in 1971, the giant Jumbo Floating Restaurant caught fire. Today, as a precautionary measure, its even more massive replacement only appears to float, while actually sitting on a concrete platform. And its incandescent glow is intentional, rather than the result of inflammatory causes.

Lord Aberdeen, for whom Aberdeen harbour is named, never saw Hong Kong as anything other than a temporary base. As Foreign Secretary, he wrote, in January 1842, to advise that Hong Kong was not to be thought of as a permanent British possession, but only as a bargaining counter, a place militarily occupied and liable to be restored to the Chinese Government on the attainment of the objects which Her Majesty's Government seek from China.

In imitation of the pharaohs of Egypt, commissioning pyramids for their afterlife, the Government ordained that Murray Building, constructed as a barracks in 1843, should not disappear from the face of the earth upon its demolition in 1983, to make way for the Bank of China Tower, but rather should be restored, stone by numbered stone, on a suitable site. That site was not determined until 15 years later, when Murray Building was resurrected on the shores of Stanley Bay.

Turn sharp right at Lion Rock, then proceed between the resettlement blocks of Kowloon City. Not directions on a road map but close to the rule of thumb advice handed by veterans to first-time pilots making the north west approach to Kai Tak airport. Much easier was the approach through Lei Yue Mun pass in the south east, affording an alignment similar to the flight path leading to Kai Tak's replacement at Chek Lap Kok.

Much water has flowed through Hong Kong harbour since liners first berthed at wharves that have long been replaced by the tiered decks of the Ocean Terminal. But the comings and goings of varied forms of transportation still enliven this tip of the Kowloon peninsula, transforming it into a launch pad for endlessly varied travel possibilities. The problems of air-conditioning for early public light buses were solved by their open-sided design.

The Kowloon peninsula might almost have been geographically configured to afford maximum convenience to the world's floating population of globetrotters. Here converged every conceivable mode of transportation short of the aeroplane. But then, by some masterstroke of unfathomable planning, the mutual dependency of this beautifully conceived infrastructure was destroyed by the removal of the railway, and its replacement by a windowless shrine to the gods of culture.

The motor car rapidly established precedence over all other accoutrements of all-important status among the Hong Kong hierarchy, whose motto has ever been. *If you can afford it, flaunt it.* Swingeing registration and transportation tax, the staggeringly high price of petrol, the lack of parking spaces and the extortionate fees charged when they can be found, serve only to enhance the appeal of car ownership as a means of asserting one's social ascendancy.

Travel was no longer the preserve of the rich and fortunate when the Peninsula Hotel opened its doors in 1928. Faster steamships, and the introduction of round-the-world cruises, had suddenly made it possible to contemplate the prospect of circumnavigating the globe with all the comforts of deck sports, on-board swimming pools, day excursions at each port of call and bridge parties after dinner in the company of like-minded fellow passengers celebrating retirement on ample pensions.

To parvenus submitting to newfound cravings for self-indulgence, and hoping to cultivate the taste to do that with some sense of style, the Peninsula looked like the apotheosis of everything to which they aspired. Perhaps seated at the next table, in the elegantly columned lounge, one might detect a vacationing movie star or peregrinating author, either of whom might be persuaded to part with an autograph if one could but summon the nerve to ask.

Long looked down upon by the Peak dwellers of Hong Kong island, Kowloon was quietly but steadily establishing its own modus vivendi in the early years of the twentieth century. Governor Sir Matthew Nathan (1904 – 1907) had caused a stir by authorizing a broad boulevard bearing his name, which he saw as the first leg of a highway to Peking. Suddenly it had become acceptable to consider living on the other side of the water, if one could only ignore the growing prevalence of tourists.

Kowloon absorbed most post-war immigrants, arriving in such numbers that enterprising developers could not put up tenement blocks fast enough to house them. Squatter settlements spread in a ramshackle rash up hillsides, vulnerable to rainstorms and especially prone to the dangers of fire. When a major conflagration consumed the makeshift township of Shek Kip Mei settlement in 1953 the government was forced to launch a resettlement programme, greatly accelerated by order of Governor Sir Murray MacLehose (insert) 1971-82.

101

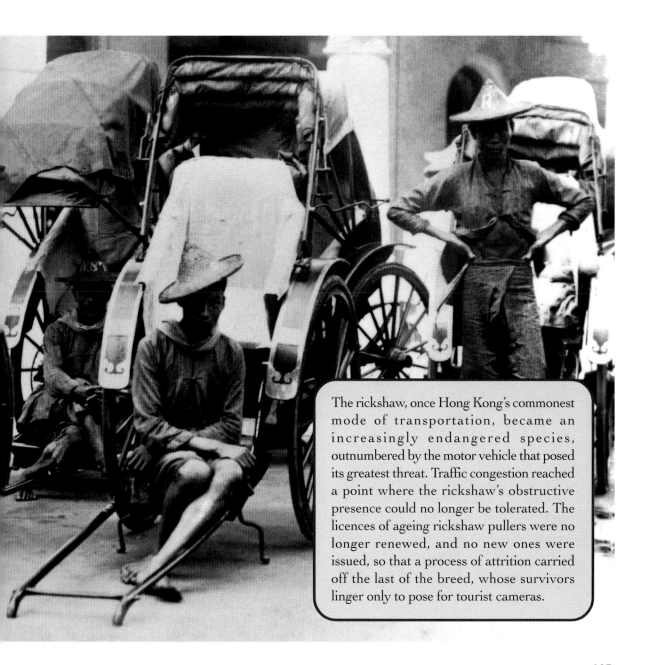

The rickshaw, once Hong Kong's commonest mode of transportation, became an increasingly endangered species, outnumbered by the motor vehicle that posed its greatest threat. Traffic congestion reached a point where the rickshaw's obstructive presence could no longer be tolerated. The licences of ageing rickshaw pullers were no longer renewed, and no new ones were issued, so that a process of attrition carried off the last of the breed, whose survivors linger only to pose for tourist cameras.

Just when it seems that cottage industries, once prolific in the alleyways and back streets of Hong Kong and Kowloon, have followed the rickshaw into extinction, a chance discovery will reveal baskets, food covers and cane hats gracing a store front that specializes in humble household implements, still assembled by hand in a time-honoured continuity of craftsmanship.

Among the most exquisite of hand-crafted products are the decorated cages hanging in a bird market where, depending on the intricacy of carving embellishing their minutest furnishings, these highly specialised forms of avian housing can exceed the cost of the occupants. True bird lovers lavish such care and attention on their pets that it is common to see the cage of some prized specimen perambulated through a public park, to be hung on the branch of a tree where the bird will sing to its heart's content.

Once extensively inundated by terraced rice fields, tilled by Asia's most eminently waterproof traction device, the mud-wallowing buffalo, the ever shrinking agricultural resources of the New Territories have contracted into a patchwork quilt of tiny vegetable gardens. These are frequently hemmed in by the high rise towers of ever-spreading satellite townships that now house nearly half of Hong Kong's total population of just under seven million.

Largely surrounded by water, Hong Kong has been driven to extremes, and considerable sums of investment, to supply its growing population with the potable variety. In the 1960's – before ambitious engineering projects carved reservoirs from the sea at Plover Cove and High Island – bouts of rationing limited town dwellers to four hours supply every four days, when patient queues formed at street taps to bear the liquid away in metal cans. Today most water is piped across the border from Guangdong Province.

Po Lin Monastery was serenely isolated in the folds of the Ngong Ping highlands on Lantau island when it first opened its doors in 1920. Started with just a shrine dedicated to Buddha, it steadily expanded, with larger halls, into a sprawling temple complex. In 1993 the world's largest outdoor Buddha was erected on the crest of a hill overlooking the complex, rapidly establishing Ngong Ping as one of the most popular tourist destinations in Hong Kong.

Where three arches once sufficed for their traditional stone ancestors in the New Territories, three bridges now facilitate the convergence of traffic bound from the western New Territories, and from the international airport on Lantau island, towards the metropolis on the shores of Hong Kong harbour. Of these outstanding architectural feats, the largest is the double-decked Tsing Ma suspension bridge and the most striking is the Ting Kau bridge spanning the Rambler Channel (seen here).